Fiona Pitt-Kethley

MINERAL ADVENTURES

Rack Press

First published in 2015 in a limited edition of one hundred and fifty copies, the first fifty numbered and signed by the author.

Copyright © The Author, 2015

The right of Fiona Pitt-Kethley to be identified as the author of this work has been asserted by her in accordance with the Copyright, Designs and Patents Act of 1988. All rights reserved.

Published in Wales by Rack Press,
The Rack, Kinnerton, Presteigne, Powys, LD8 2PF
Tel: 01547 560 411
All orders and correspondence: rackpress@nicholasmurray.co.uk

ISBN 978-0-9927654-9-1

Printed by Artisan Print, Presteigne, Powys

The Opal Menilites of Agramón

Bright yellow broomrape bursting from the clay,
close to the minerals we're searching for.
Nothing's what you'd expect in Agramón.

Blue-grey on grey at first they look discreet
and crisp as sugared almonds in the walls
until we marvel at their varied forms.
This quarry's the sex-shop of the mineral scene:
Willendorf Venuses, testicles, dicks
beside more toy-like marbles, skittles, ducks
and half-formed pre-pubescent young girls' breasts.

A heavenly jest, perhaps. Exuberant,
tumescent, waiting in their matrixes.
If stones could speak these ones would say to me:
"Release us on an unsuspecting world…"

Gypsum, Pilar de Jarabia

Close to the railway on low-lying hills
amongst the ruins of old mines and works
the spoils contain gypsum as clear as glass,
crusted along the sides with siderite,
glittering, dusty and as black as coal.
Nature's own slides for microscopes.
The gypsum shards have captured celestine,
whiter transparency within its ice.
Like flies in amber, trapped eternally,
the crystals lie pinioned within the layers.

Jacinth from Chella, Valencia

Small olive groves and orchards by a stream…
The fruit we're after is a different sort,
jacinth of Compostela, matt red quartz.
No need to chisel it from solid rock.
It lies, scattered like pips across the ground,
pineapple clusters and biterminates.
A stream becomes a river further on
where larger stones are known, unreachable
behind the curtain of a waterfall.
Parched in the sun, we sit on hardened ground,
and feast on pomegranates, dropping seeds.

Selenite
Fuentes del Ebro, Zaragoza

We've driven through a strangely surreal land
where hams hang drying in the mid-day sun
and storks' nests, jerry-built, adorn the roofs.

We reach our destination in the end:
squat alabaster igloo snowmen shapes
across a dusty plain of greyish white.
Look closely where they glister in the sun
and find the tiny shards of selenite

Acicular Aragonite, Pantoja, Toledo

The eggshell blue clay bears a type that's white.
The peachy brown reveals the orange sort.
Prickly as urchins, tiny starry-spined,
sitting in their clay matrix till they're found.
Some roll out coated with a layer of brown.
We call these "Kinder eggs".
Place in a glass of water and the earth dissolves.
A masterpiece emerges from the silt,
or not, for some are hollow, worthless shells.

Deviline

A friend was the first man in Spain to find
a micro-mineral called deviline.
Something about its name attracted me.
It sounded fairly devilish to find.
I pledged to be the second getting it.
Each Sunday I would walk the quarry paths,
searching amongst the other copper minerals,
taking a jeweller's loupe to magnify.

Our friend found his in Corta Gloria,
The quarry where ETA terrorists hid out
after they'd bombed the Guardia, taking lives.
I found it in San Jose, long disused,
a quarry planned to take the residues
that now contaminate the Portmán beach.
I rescued all the samples that I could
before the tippers can obscure this part.

Just faintly greenish to the naked eye,
a little fibrous underneath a loupe,
less crystalline than malachite found there.
I viewed it with a microscope, back home,
Another world appears when magnified,
caverns of stone, with folds of siderite,
sparkles of chalcopyrite, sceptred quartz.
I lose myself within this other world.

**Erythrite (hydrated cobalt arsenate)
Cerro Minado, Huercal Overa.**

Easy to recognise amongst these stones,
a *femme fatale*, loaded with arsenic,
rose madder, cupcake icing, Barbie pink.

No wildlife living in this silent spot.
Some pines grow here but little else it seems.
A garden fit for Mithridates' use.
The flies of Andalusia can't survive.
A woodpigeon has fallen on its breast.

What happened to the miners who worked here?
Two or three hours were quite enough for us…
Did they die young? Or else grow used to it,
weathering the poison as Rasputin did?

Seductive, toxic femininity.
We view its deadly beauty through a loupe.
I mistrust women and minerals in pink.
More manicure than heart, deadly at core.

Apatite
La Celia, Jumilla

Bats live here. In the day they're all asleep,
silently, upside down, hanging in pairs.
Reminds me of a tale I told my son,
set in a ghost train with three skeletons
and bats "Mr and Mrs Dracula".

The mine's walls are of warm grey jumillite
Hematite glitters everywhere in sight.
We're looking for a smaller, rarer stone.
Sat by the gridded entrance in half-light
I break up rocks to find what lies inside:
small micro crystals of green apatite,
beautifully clear, the colour of cats' eyes.

Pyrites from Navajun

Who cut them? People ask. They can't believe
geometry appears in Nature too.
These perfect cubes defy their common sense
Others insist this iron is silver or gold.

And I remember staying in Navajun.
Eight people in the village where we lodged,
outnumbered by the sheep kept in one house.

Pedro, a miner once, turned millionaire.
Now owns the quarry where he used to work,
the spot where pyrites just like these occur,
where modern miners pay to gather rocks,
where dinosaurs once walked and left their prints.

It's June but freezing in the mountain air.
Stone houses built with massy walls spread cold.
The quarry's higher still. We warm with work,
hammering cavelets into damp grey walls.
laying our spoils in trays that once held fruit.

It's time to leave. The cars drive down a road,
rocky and half-destroyed by lorryloads.
Tired, cold and happy, we devour our food…
artichokes simmered with wine, tomatoes, herbs
and tiny fragments of Serrano ham,
chistorras, little spicy sausages.
lamb chops barbecued over vine wood chips,
large juicy heart-shaped cherries from nearby.
And all washed down with fine Rioja wine.

Hornblende from Carboneras

A town once big on coal, out on a limb,
reached one way by a hellish coastal road
with death-defying drops along its route.
It's just got tourism now, tourism and fish.
As we drove in an angler walking by
was carrying a swordfish shouldered on a sling.

The hornblende, I had heard, was out of town
beside the Algarobica beach,
whose deserts of speckled sands and rolling dunes
were used in Lawrence of Arabia scenes.
A Spanish Tower of Babel dominates,
a relic of the building boom gone bust,
when nature was attacked on every front.
It's many storeys high, a vast hotel,
without a room to let to passers-by.
condemned before its final plastering,
reaching for heaven, a vast white elephant.
A fence keeps any would-be squatters out.

The rocks I want are all along the road,
no rarity, the local building stone,
grey andesite spotted with crystals, brownish black.
Hornblende's a name of ugly homeliness
that pairs with horn-rimmed glasses in my mind